K-POP

Sierra Wilson

MY FAVORITE MUSIC

AV2

www.openlightbox.com

AV2

Step 1
Go to **www.openlightbox.com**

Step 2
Enter this unique code

ZHDNCJRI1

Step 3
Explore your interactive eBook!

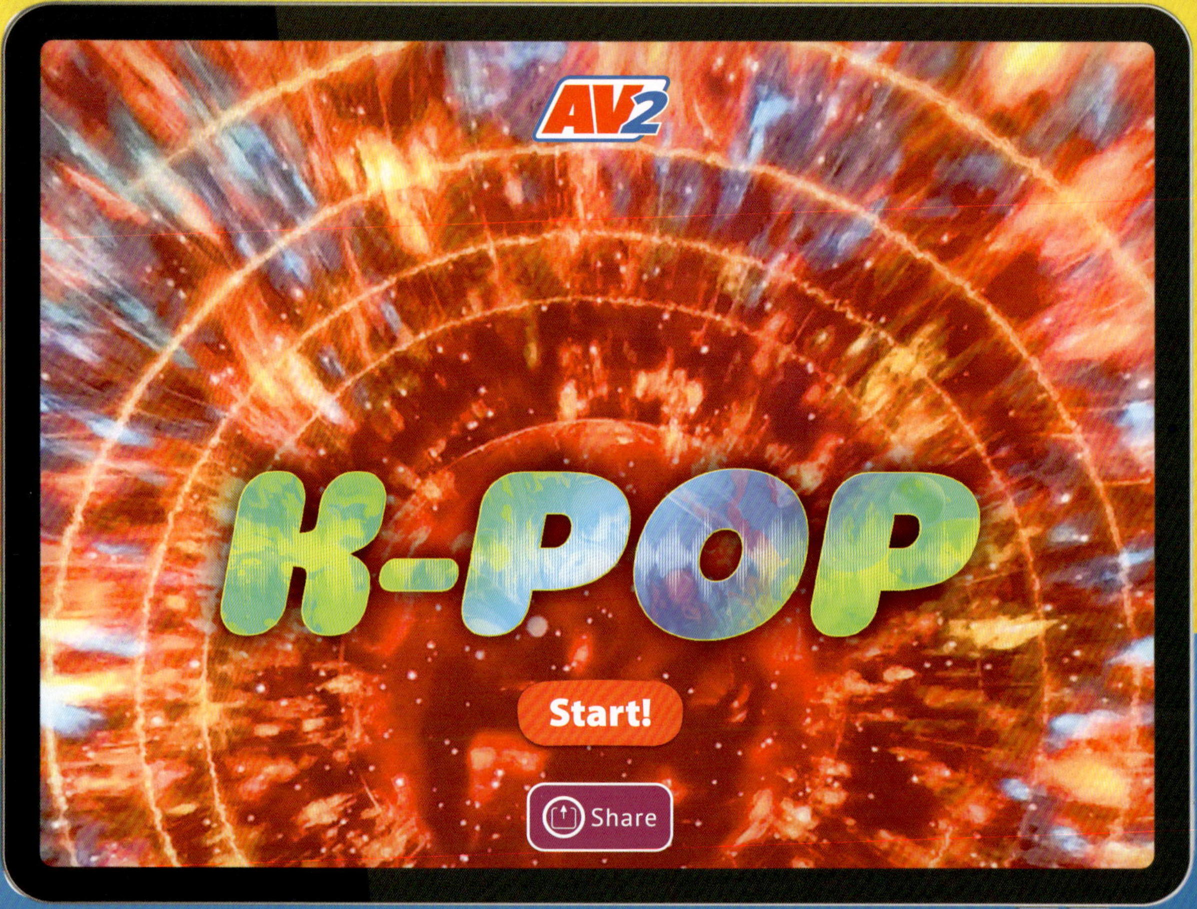

Your interactive eBook comes with...

AV2 is optimized for use on any device

- Read — **Audio**: Listen to the entire book read aloud
- **Videos**: Watch informative video clips
- **Weblinks**: Gain additional information for research
- **Try This!**: Complete activities and hands-on experiments
- **Key Words**: Study vocabulary, and complete a matching word activity
- **Quizzes**: Test your knowledge
- **Slideshows**: View images and captions
- **Share**: Share titles within your Learning Management System (LMS) or Library Circulation System
- **Citation**: Create bibliographical references following APA, CMOS, and MLA styles

This title is part of our AV2 digital subscription

1-Year K–5 Subscription
ISBN 978-1-7911-3320-7

Access hundreds of AV2 titles with our digital subscription.
Sign up for a FREE trial at **www.openlightbox.com/trial**

The digital components of this book are guaranteed to stay active for at least five years from the date of publication.

K-POP

Contents

2 Interactive eBook Code
4 When Did K-Pop Start?
6 Where Did K-Pop Come From?
8 Early K-Pop Artists
10 Singing K-Pop
12 What Are K-Pop Songs About?
14 Instruments
16 In a Band
18 K-Pop Today
20 I Love K-Pop Music
22 K-Pop Facts
24 Sight Words

I love music.

K-pop is my favorite kind of music.

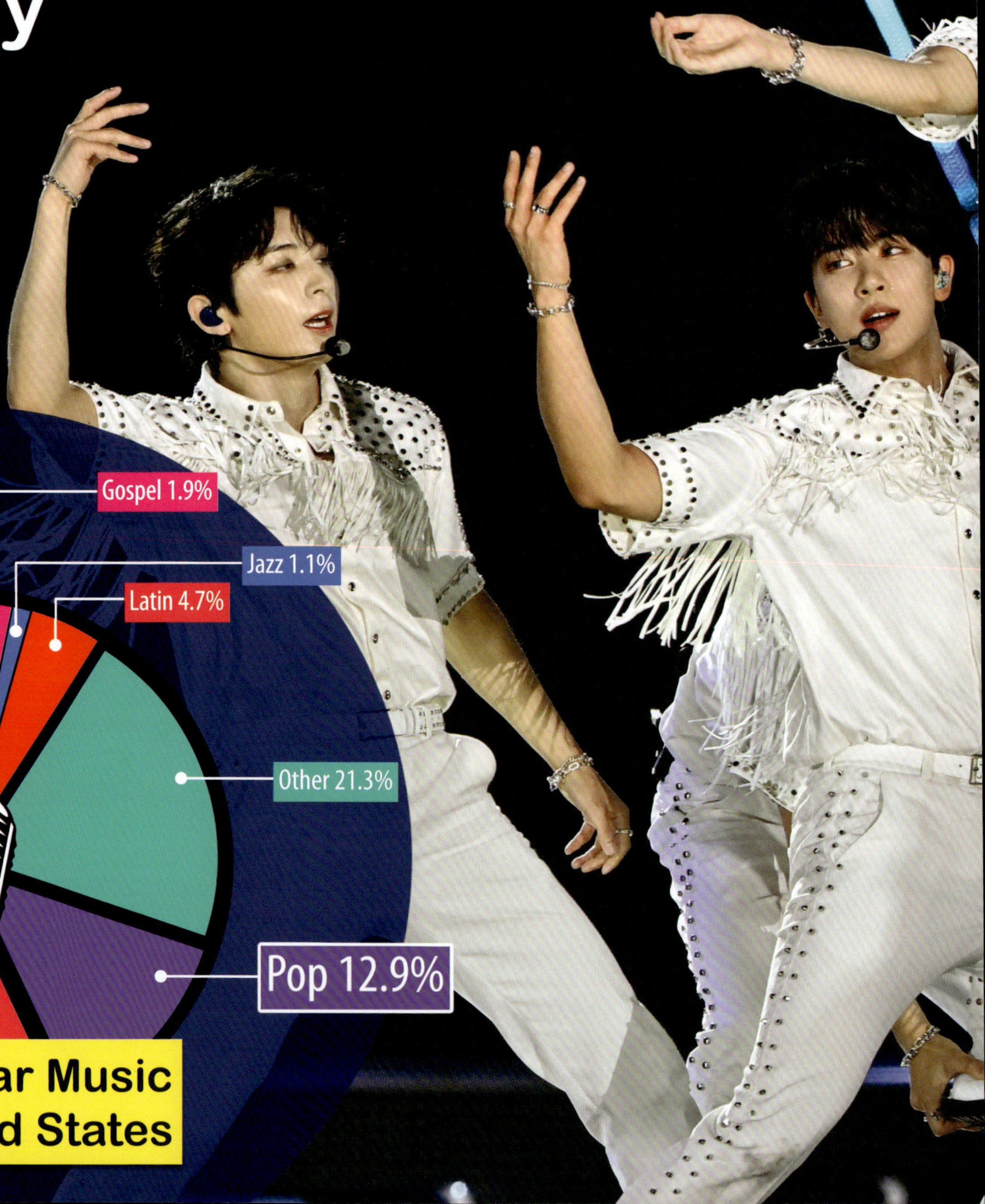

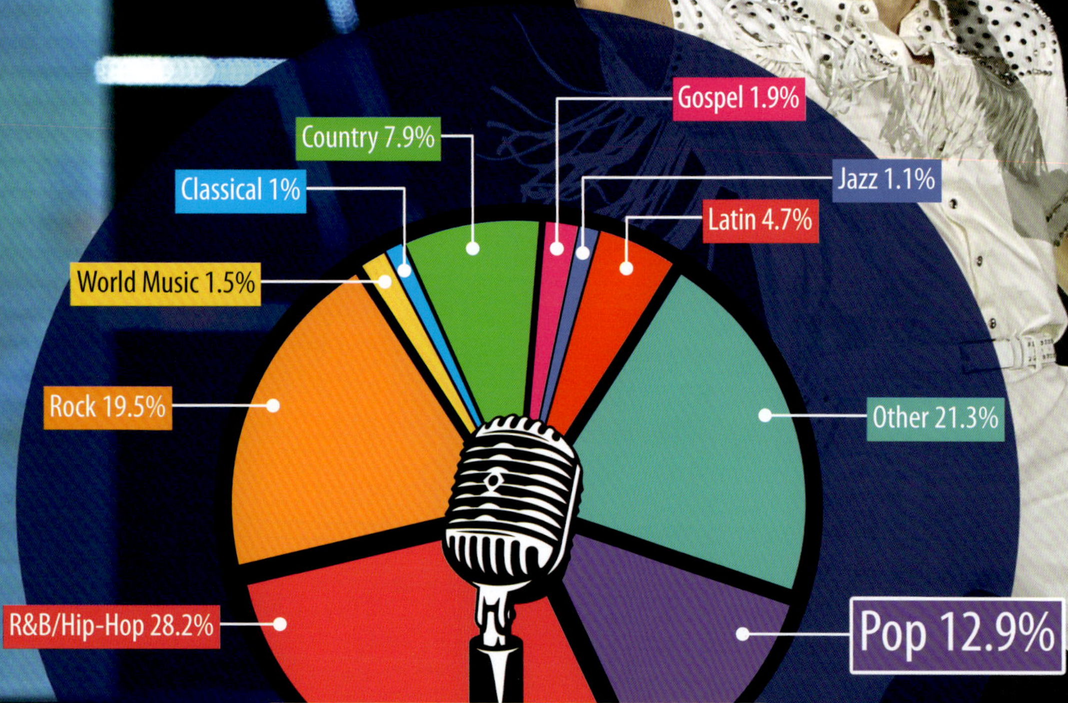

Most Popular Music in the United States

The first K-pop music was made in South Korea in the early 1990s.

K-pop is another way to say "Korean pop."

This music mixes Korean and American pop music.

K-pop songs often include hip-hop, rock, and dance music as well.

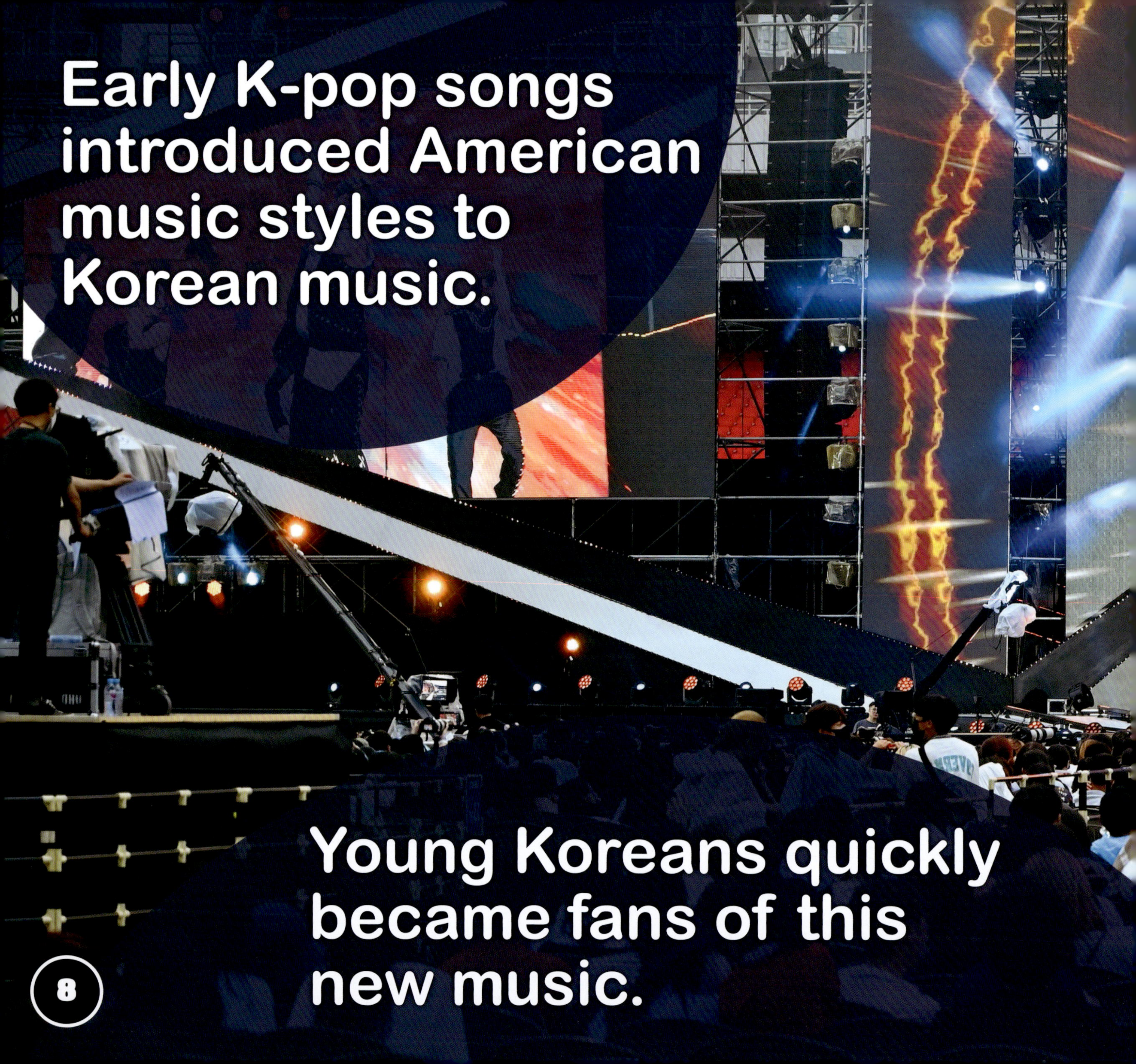

Early K-pop songs introduced American music styles to Korean music.

Young Koreans quickly became fans of this new music.

Seo Taiji and Boys was the first-ever K-pop band.

K-pop singers often sing in groups.

They sing some parts of the song together and other parts on their own.

Some singers may even rap the words of the song.

Many K-pop songs are about having fun and being in love.

They make people want to dance.

Some songs talk about problems, such as bullying.

People often use computers to help make K-pop music.

Some songs include Korean instruments, such as the geomungo.

I like to sing K-pop music with my friends.

We take turns singing different parts.

Singing as a group teaches us how to work together.

Seoul, South Korea's capital city, is known as the home of K-pop.

Most K-pop singers train there.

In 2023, K-pop artists produced 5 of the year's 10 top-selling albums.

I love K-pop music.

It makes me feel good about myself.

K-POP FACTS

These pages provide detailed information that expands on the interesting facts found in the book. They are intended to be used by adults as a learning support to help young readers round out their knowledge of each musical genre featured in the *My Favorite Music* series.

Pages 4–5

I love music. K-pop is my favorite kind of music. Music is the name given to sounds made with voices or musical instruments and put together in a way that conveys emotion. People use music to express themselves. Since the 1990s, K-pop has grown in popularity. It is especially popular with young listeners.

Pages 6–7

K-pop is another way to say "Korean pop." This kind of music combines American styles of pop music with Korean music. K-pop often has a quicker rhythm and shorter verses than American music, and will include styles such as hip-hop, rap, and rock in its presentation. Like American pop music, K-pop is produced with dancing in mind. K-pop performers often have elaborate dance routines for each song they sing.

Pages 8–9

Early K-pop songs introduced American music styles to Korean music. Following the Korean War, American soldiers were stationed in South Korea. Their music became popular with the locals, and American sounds slowly began to appear in Korean music. Seo Taiji and Boys is considered the first K-pop band. They launched their act on a South Korean talent show. While the judges gave them a low score, the group caught the attention of Korea's youth. As Seo Taiji and Boys became more popular, other groups, such as H.O.T., formed and began playing in a similar style. Over time, music companies began to form their own K-pop bands.

Pages 10–11

K-pop singers often sing in groups. The song lyrics are often a combination of Korean and English words. While they sing together as a group, each member of a K-pop group typically has a section of the song he or she sings solo. Some songs also feature a rap section for performers who specialize in that area. K-pop groups also typically have people in assigned roles. These can include main singer, main rapper, and main dancer.

Pages 12–13

Many K-pop songs are about having fun and being in love. K-pop songs are known for their positivity. They often talk about experiences that fans will recognize and understand. Even if a song takes on a serious topic, such as bullying, the message will remain upbeat, letting listeners know that problems can be overcome. The music itself tends to have an infectious beat that encourages people to dance.

Pages 14–15

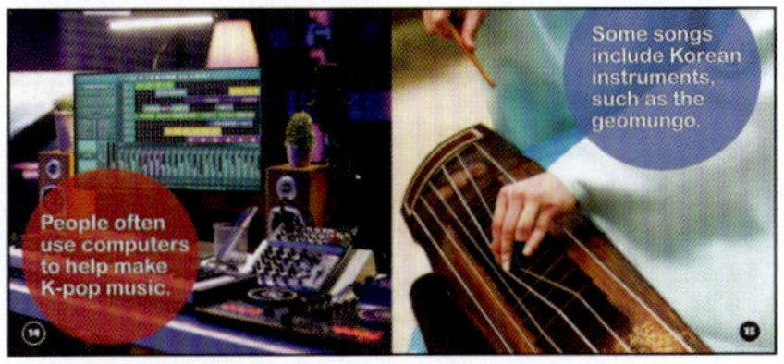

People often use computers to help make K-pop music. The background music that accompanies K-pop singers is often produced electronically, using instruments such as synthesizers and drum machines. Traditional instruments, such as pianos and guitars, can sometimes be heard as well. Some K-pop even uses traditional Korean instruments such as the *geomungo* or *haegeum* to add a cultural element to the music.

Pages 16–17

I like to sing K-pop music with my friends. Creating music with others helps teach children cooperation, teamwork, and how to achieve goals. Children who regularly play music tend to have more confidence and get along better with others. Some students learn better in groups because they do not feel the pressure of having to learn on their own.

Pages 18–19

Seoul, South Korea's capital city, is known as the home of K-pop. Seoul is the capital city of South Korea. It is the country's largest city, with a population of almost 10 million. Gangnam, a district of Seoul, is the heart of South Korea's entertainment industry. It is often referred to as "the birthplace of K-pop," as it is here that many of the country's top music companies have offices and create their K-pop groups.

Pages 20–21

I love K-pop music. Recent studies suggest that learning and practicing music can be beneficial to a child's ability to learn. Among these benefits are improved motor skills and dexterity, increased test scores, and even raised Intelligence Quotient, or IQ, scores. Learning music at an early age has also been shown to aid in language development and to improve reading and listening skills.

SIGHT WORDS

Research has shown that as much as 65 percent of all written material published in English is made up of 300 words. These 300 words cannot be taught using pictures or learned by sounding them out. They must be recognized by sight. This book contains 67 common sight words to help young readers improve their reading fluency and comprehension. This book also teaches young readers several important content words. These words are paired with pictures to aid in learning and improve understanding.

Page	Sight Words First Appearance
4	country, I, in, is, kind, most, my, of, other, states, the, world
5	first, made, was
6	American, and, another, say, this, to, way
7	as, often, songs, well
8	new, young
10	groups, on, own, parts, some, their, they, together
11	even, may, words
12	about, are, being, make, many, people
13	such, talk, want
14	help, use
16	different, like, take, turns, we, with
17	a, how, us, work
18	city, home, there
19	year
21	good, it, me

Page	Content Words First Appearance
4	classical, gospel, hip-hop, jazz, K-pop, Latin, music, pop, R&B, rock, United States
5	South Korea
8	fans, styles
9	band, Seo Taiji and Boys
12	fun, love
13	bullying, problems
14	computers
15	geomungo, instruments
16	friends
18	Seoul
19	albums, artists

Published by Lightbox Learning Inc.
276 5th Avenue, Suite 704 #917
New York, NY 10001
Website: www.openlightbox.com

Library of Congress Cataloging-in-Publication Data
Names: Wilson, Sierra, author.
Title: K-pop / Sierra Wilson.
Description: New York : Lightbox Learning Inc., 2026. | Series: My favorite music | Audience: Grades 2-3
Identifiers: LCCN 2024048451 (print) | LCCN 2024048452 (ebook) | ISBN 9798874503833 (library binding) | ISBN 9798874503840 (paperback) | ISBN 9798874503857 (ebook other) | ISBN 9798874515256 (ebook other)
Subjects: LCSH: Popular music--Korea (South)--History and criticism--Juvenile literature.
Classification: LCC ML3502.K6 W55 2025 (print) | LCC ML3502.K6 (ebook) | DDC 781.63095195--dc23/eng/20241015
LC record available at https://lccn.loc.gov/2024048451
LC ebook record available at https://lccn.loc.gov/2024048452

Printed in Guangzhou, China
1 2 3 4 5 6 7 8 9 0 29 28 27 26 25

042025
100924

Art Director: Terry Paulhus **Project Coordinator:** Heather Kissock